ISBN 978-1-334-92775-1
PIBN 10782544

1 MONTH OF
FREE
READING

at

www.ForgottenBooks.com

By purchasing this book you are eligible for one month membership to ForgottenBooks.com, giving you unlimited access to our entire collection of over 1,000,000 titles via our web site and mobile apps.

To claim your free month visit: www.forgottenbooks.com/free782544

English
Français
Deutsche
Italiano
Español
Português

www.forgottenbooks.com

Mythology Photography **Fiction**
Fishing Christianity **Art** Cooking
Essays Buddhism Freemasonry
Medicine **Biology** Music **Ancient
Egypt** Evolution Carpentry Physics
Dance Geology **Mathematics** Fitness
Shakespeare **Folklore** Yoga Marketing
Confidence Immortality Biographies
Poetry **Psychology** Witchcraft
Electronics Chemistry History **Law**
Accounting **Philosophy** Anthropology
Alchemy Drama Quantum Mechanics
Atheism Sexual Health **Ancient History**
Entrepreneurship Languages Sport
Paleontology Needlework Islam
Metaphysics Investment Archaeology
Parenting Statistics Criminology
Motivational

Microreproductions / Institut canadien de microreproductions historiques

1987

The Institute has attempted to obtain the best original copy available for filming. Features of this copy which may be bibliographically unique, which may alter any of the images in the reproduction, or which may significantly change the usual method of filming, are checked below.

L'Institut a micr- qu'il lui a été po- de cet exemplair- point de vue bib- une image repro- modification da- sont indiqués ci-

☑ Coloured covers/
Couverture de couleur

☐ Covers damaged/
Couverture endommagée

☐ Covers restored and/or laminated/
Couverture restaurée et/ou pelliculée

☐ Cover title missing/
Le titre de couverture manque

☐ Coloured maps/
Cartes géographiques en couleur

☐ Coloured ink (i.e. other than blue or black)/
Encre de couleur (i.e. autre que bleue ou noire)

☐ Coloured plates and/or illustrations/
Planches et/ou illustrations en couleur

☐ Bound with other material/
Relié avec d'autres documents

☐ Tight binding may cause shadows or distortion along interior margin/
La reliure serrée peut causer de l'ombre ou de la distorsion le long de la marge intérieure

☐ Blank leaves added during restoration may appear within the text. Whenever possible, these have been omitted from filming/
Il se peut que certaines pages blanches ajoutées lors d'une restauration apparaissent dans le texte, mais, lorsque cela était possible, ces pages n'ont pas été filmées.

☐ Additional comments:/
Commentaires supplémentaires:

☐ Coloured p
Pages de c

☐ Pages dam
Pages endc

☐ Pages resto
Pages resta

☑ Pages discc
Pages déco

☑ Pages detae
Pages détae

☑ Showthrou
Transparene

☐ Quality of p
Qualité iné

☐ Includes su
Comprend

☐ Only edition
Seule éditio

☐ Pages whol
slips, tissues
ensure the b
Les pages to
obscurcies p
etc., ont été
obtenir la m

HALI

"ITS SINS AN

APRIL

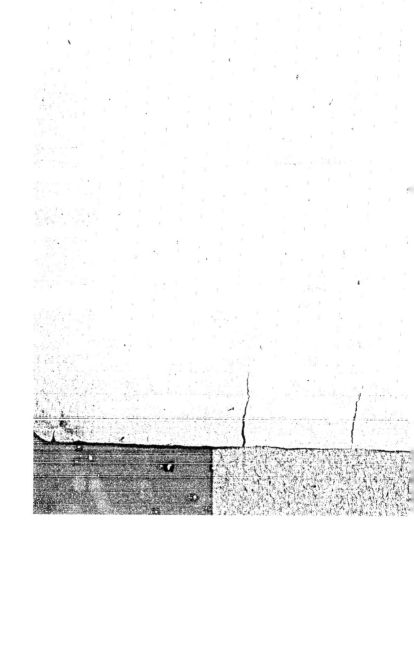

HALIFAX:

" ITS SINS AND SORROWS."

⸺⸺⸺

"If .thou forbear to deliver them that are drawn unto death, and those that are ready to be slain; if thou sayest, Behold, we knew it not; doth not He that pondereth the heart consider it? and He that keepeth thy soul, doth He not know it? and shall not He render to every man according to his works."—PROVERBS, XXIV. 11, 12.

. APRIL 9, 1862.

⸺⸺⸺

HALIFAX, N. S.:
CONFERENCE JOB PRINTING OFFICE.
1862.

1544

fi
n
tl
w
a
a
a
.
S
a
is
m
th

al
d
th
pr

Halifax,—"Its Sins and Sorrows:"

None, probably, will controvert this statement, that, in general, cities are centres of light and of darkness—centres of virtue and centres of vice. That such should be the case is natural. To account for it is easy.

In large cities vast numbers of the human family are congregated together. These we may regard as separating by common consent into two classes, one of which we may label Virtuous, and the other Vicious. Many belonging to the first mentioned class endeavor to obey the two great commandments—"Thou shalt love the Lord thy God with all thy heart, and with all thy soul, and with all thy mind, and with all thy strength;" and "Thou shalt love thy neighbor as thyself."—Mark xii. 30, 31. Others make a feeble effort at obedience; but their hobbling gait and frequent stumbles are proofs positive that they find it rather difficult to walk · in all the statutes and ordinances of the Lord blameless." Still upon the whole these manage in some way to keep up an appearance of the virtuous and the good, and though "it is not all gold that glitters," still the glittering which they make adds, in human estimation, a lustre to the pure gold of the sanctuary.

Those who may be properly denominated *vicious*, are not all equally so. Many of them are very decent persons in daylight, and they would not by any means let the sun see them handing over their contributions to a poison vender, a procuress, or any other personification of vice. Yet the sum

total of such contributions keep in the same condition the
" Moral Wastes" of cities. In the same condition? There
is no such thing, in a moral point of view. People are either
becoming better or worse daily. There is no moral neutral
ground, no standing still—"evil men and seducers wax
worse and worse."—2 Tim. iii. 13. As they wax worse
and worse, so does thy wrath of Almighty God wax hotter
and hotter, and the arrows of His vengeance fly thicker and
faster around them. At length, having reached the limits of
his endurance, "darts strike through their livers," Prov. vii.
23, and they are hurled into that hell which has been long
gaping for them, whence " the smoke of their torment ascends
forever and ever."—Rev. xiv. 11.

In a city many opportunities are afforded the virtuous for
improving their own spiritual condition and advancing schemes
of philanthropy and Christian benevolence. But, alas! in
cities, too, the number, the diversity, the deceitfulness, and
the potency of the inventions and wiles of men and devils, or
rather of men-devils and women-devils, for ensnaring the
unwary, and, when fairly ensnared, of ruining their hapless
victims for society, for time and eternity, are quite appalling.
To such an extent is th's the case that all the moral force which
can be mustered in most large cities is scarcely sufficient to
keep at bay the advancing legions of the devil and his emissa-
ries. That cities become centres of virtue and centres of vice
is accounted for on the principle of *sympathy of numbers*.

London, e. g., is the greatest city in the world: it is the
world's Capital. It is the Bible Depository of nations. One
Society alone issues nearly *four millions* of the Sacred Scrip-
tures annually; and yet within an easy walk of Charing
Cross are miles and miles of lanes and alleys, on either side
of London Bridge, where the people are living in atheism and
heathenism, and with moral perceptions so blunted, with the
religious element in their souls so seared and scorched by
liquid fire, that they are almost wholly disqualified for

perceiving the difference between right and wrong. Every
noble aspiration is crushed, and every generous feeling is
burnt out of their souls. All honor to those who have been
hasting to the rescue.

Having made these preliminary remarks, let us now proceed to mention some of the "Sins and Sorrows" of Halifax.
Let us then take a fair and pitying look at

HALIFAX,—"ITS SINS AND SORROWS."

and may the sight affect our eyes; our eyes our hearts; and
our hearts our lips and hands.

Iniquity abounds in Halifax,—"As ashamed" it *does not*
"hide its head." Let us commence by taking a look at its

SABBATH DESECRATION.

There are two commandments in the Decalogue more jea-
lously guarded, so to speak, than any of the others, viz: the
Fourth and the Tenth. He who "needed not that any
should testify of man, for he knew what was in man,"
was fully aware that peculiar temptations would arise in the
ordinary course of events, to induce men to violate the Fourth
and Tenth commandments. *Covetousness*—the procuring
cause of a vast proportion of existing wretchedness and crime
—would be ever ready to lay its avaricious hands upon the
Tenth, and not upon the Tenth only, but upon the Fourth
also: yea, upon the entire code. The effects produced by
grasping, grinding avariciousness, in the thousand forms of
over-reaching, defrauding and double dealing, which it as-
sumes, and which frequently lead to open robbery, destruction and death, are clearly visible, and but too palpable.
And with shame and confusion of face Christians are forced
to acknowledge that it is a crying sin, if not *the* sin of the
Church. "The love of money is the root of all evil."—1
Tim. vi. 10.

As regards the law of the Sabbath, many and pointed are the warnings of God in His Word against its infraction. It is placed in the body of the Decalogue, and in addition is hedged round by numerous special precepts,—" Verily my My Sabbaths ye shall keep: for it is a sign between me and and you throughout your generations ; that ye may know that I am the Lord that do sanctify you,"—" Ye shall keep my Sabbaths, and reverence my santuary : I am the Lord."— Lev. xxvi. 2. "In earing time and harvest thou shalt rest." —Ex. xxxiv. 21. Now, why all this precaution on God's part? Because he has declared " I AM THE LORD." But the daring violator of *His* day, had he power, would dethrone the Lord of heaven and earth.

Even in this life, signal and tremendous have been God's vindications of the honor and sanctity of His own day. Numerous are the recorded instances of individuals and companies having been visited in hot displeasure while desecrating the Lord's Day, and hurried away unprepared into an awful eternity : but many despise reproof and will not take warning.

Halifax, like other Garrison Towns is obliged to contend with the demoralizing influences of a depraved soldiery— among those, however, are honorable exceptions. Most of the Military commanders who have been from time to time stationed in this city have given the weight of their influence towards helping on Sabbath profanation, by allowing their soldiers to march to and from Church on the Lord's day to the sound of martial music. Much of that music was not so martial either, for there is not much of the spirit of Mars in " Dixie Land," " There's nae luck about the House," or " Old Dan. Tucker," &c. These air, however, played by a fine band, did not fail to attract crowds of the lower orders, and in such numbers as to nearly block up the streets and side-walks opposite the Garrison Chapel. After submitting to this outrage on the sanctity of the Lord's Day, and on the feelings of many Christians who feared God and reverenced the Sabbath, an effort was made to have it suppressed. "Old Dan. Tucker" began to sound so flat to ears attuned to sacred melody, that it became intolerable. The lovers of the Sabbath, putting their heads together, as the saying is, approached General Doyle very respectfully and said:— "General Doyle can't you oblige us by keeping 'Old Dan.' at home on the Sabbath?" "Certainly," said the good General: and so "Old Dan. Tucker" has not been to Church ever since.

We may next notice the plying of the Ferry Boats between the City and Dartmouth, from morning till ten or eleven o'clock at night, excepting during the time of Divine Service. These are run *professedly* to oblige a few of the good folk in Dartmouth, who prefer worshipping in the City; but we believe the *real object* is to make money and accommodate a multitude of Sabbath-despising pleasure seekers. At any rate there is a whole establishment kept up 365 days in the year, —men in the boats, and men on either side to receive money and supply tickets. Well, we cannot see why the Trains, for similar reasons, should not run on the Sabbath. Whatever feelings of compunction of conscience Christian commons-to-and-fro may have first felt when they committed themselves to this species of Sabbath profanation, they have been since bravely overcome, for so indispensable are they now regarded that even Ministers of the Gospel pray publicly for the welfare of this God-dishonoring convenience.

> "Vice is a monster of such hideous mien
> As to be hated need but to be seen;
> But seen too oft, familiar with her face,
> We first endure, then pity, then embrace."

Again, when the Mail Steamers come in on the Sabbath, Cunard's wharf is crowded with men, omnibusses and trucks, and for the time being there is no more Sabbath than there is in Paris.

Winter and summer, too, the milkmen are allowed to hawk
milk through the town, from house to house. The quiet and
rest of the Sab' ath is disturbed in a variety of ways, and with
as much impunity as though there was not one word in the
Bible, or one enactment in the Statute Book respecting the
observance of the Lord's day. But lest any should feel dis-
posed to doubt or deny that the state of things is so bad, let
us summon some veracious witnesses to bear testimony to our
statements.

The first City Missionary, Gordon, commenced his labors
as such in Halifax, in 1852. In his Report, written in
1854, he thus speaks: "Most of those children," (when
children do such things fancy what they will be capable of
when they attain the years of majority), "Most of those
children who break the hallowed silence of the Lord's Day
and give way to their hellish oaths and blasphemous talk, to
the great annoyance of Protestant families in different parts
of the City, are of Roman Catholic parentage. In viewing
with horror the infamous conduct of such youths on the Lord's
Day I have asked myself this question, 'Are the Magistrates
and Justices of the Peace justifiers of these disturbances?'
Surely he is not worthy the name of Justice of the Peace
who puts forth no efforts to preserve that peace which every
citizen, in accordance with the law of our land, has a right to
enjoy on the Lord's Day."

That is true; but bad as these thing are we shall now mention something more startling still :—The Fish Market is
kept open on Sabbath mornings *by enactment*. We are informed by a legal authority that the laws respecting the opening of the Fish Market and the running of the Ferry Boats
on Sabbath are not local but general, and the same things
may be done in any part of Nova Scotia. Here then are
Provincial enactments for Sabbath desecration. Look at that
ye come-day-go-day Nova Scotians! And you, ye professors
of the Christian name, who with your lips sometimes loudly

extol the *Lord of the Sabbath*, why do ye tamely submit to
these outrages? Ye allow the godless to trample His Day
under their feet, and, as if that was not enough, some of you
assist them in helping on the work of Sabbath desecration.

"I may state," adds the Missionary, "that by my Sabbath-day visits I have ascertained that there is a large quan-
tity of property sold in this city on the Lord's Day, especially
at the seasons of Spring and Autumn, which it is worthy of
noticing is sold during the hours in which the legal authorities
allow the Fish Market to be opened, at 9 o'clock. When I
have pled with the keepers of groceries and other venders at
wharves for the law of the Sabbath they referred me to this
wicked example as being of legal authority, and contended
for the same privilege. Surely if these things were rightly
brought under the notice of those who are the means of keeping the Fish Market open on the Lord's Day, they would
not be so heathenish as not to refrain from setting such an
example as, ultimately, will bring upon them such an amount
of guilt as any reasonable men should deprecate."

Well, we will only add, that in this year of our Lord one
thousand eight hundred and *sixty two!* the Fish Market is
still open on Sabbath; and so indifferent have the professing people of God in this City become about the sanctity of
the Lord's Day that we believe one half of them do not know
it. Indeed so indifferent in general had the citizens of Halifax become about the interests of the Sabbath, that no later
than the winter of 1861 a poor fellow of mushroom growth
and duration, as it happened, started up, thrust his unholy
hand into the Ark of the Covenant, dragged out the Book of
the Law, and, having erased the Fourth Commandment,
stumped the whole City, with all its Ministers, Sabbath lovers
and observers, to prove that men were under any obligation
to "remember the Sabbath Day and keep it holy." What
was to be done? There was a formidable Anti-Sabbatarian
suddenly sprung up, and with a formidable force to back him.

His information, too, was extensive and his erudition profound, for he knew Alpha from Omega, and Lambda from Lithgow; and the profundity of his arguments was only surpassed by his *ad captandum* eloquence. He held forth in Temperance Hall, to an enraptured audience, which, in the exuberance of its joy, shouted, "Hurrah for the man that gives us one Commandment less to keep, and adds one more day to the week! Hurrah!" A layman, however, made an honest and successful attempt at keeping sacriligious hands off the sa‑ cred institution of the Sabbath, but the many were too much for the one, and the few, who having one by one silently re‑ tired, the many were showed the doors by the man who at‑ tended to the gasometer. But this circumstance served to enhance the lustre of the luminary; who needed not any more light thrown upon his subject than what himself could supply, and the glow-worm is always known by its spark.

It was discovered, however, that "tho' beaten he could argue still;" and subsequently a clergyman condescended to enter the lists with Goldsmith's Village Schoolmaster. The precaution though was this time taken of getting the Mayor to act as Chairman of the meeting, and of having a Police force on hand. The Hall was crowded. The meet‑ ing was orderly. The issue was not doubtful, for the Anti-Sabbatarian, the disturber of the equanimity of the commu‑ nity, immediately after sunk down into his original obscurity, whence he has not since emerged.

The playing of the Military Band in this City on Sabbath, for so many years, the licensing of Milk-men, the plying of the Ferry Boats—on which account Dartmouth in particular suffers, as it is made a Sabbath-day rioting ground—the desecration of the Lord's Day when the Mail Steamer arrives, and that consequent upon the opening of the Fish Market, such as the selling of property, &c.—all these things, and others unmentioned, afford abundant and painful proofs of the religious effeminacy of the Lord's professed people in the City of Halifax.

A few years ago an effort was made by the Sabbath Alliance—which, with the House of Refuge, are now numbered with the good things that were—to ascertain in so far as possible the amount of Sabbath desecration in and around Halifax. The following is an account of the results of that investigation. All, or nearly all the instances of profanation mentioned occurred within the short space of *two or three* hours. The testimony of the present City Missionary, who has been laboring as such for six years, is, that the City is now in a worse moral condition than when he commenced his labors.

STATEMENT OF SABBATH DESECRATION IN AND AROUND HALIFAX.

1. "The greater proportion of the houses licensed for the sale of spirituous liquors in Barrack, Albermarle, Grafton, and Water Streets, sell these liquors on Sabbath. Last Sabbath, between 3 and 5 o'clock, p. m., spirituous liquors could have been purchased in *Thirty-six shops.*

2. "The Fish Market is open from 6 to 9 o'clock, a. m. Last Sabbath, between 7 and 8 o'clock, a. m., there were twenty-six stalls with Fish, nine boats afloat, and four on the slip; one hundred and seventy-four persons purchased fish between 7 and 8 o'clock.

3. "Last Sabbath Vessels were selling Potatoes at head of Wharf.

4. "At the same hour, between 7 and 8 o'clock, six Butcher Shops were open, and meat sold.

5. "On Sabbath, the 11th of this month, there were not less that forty individuals seen angling on the Lakes on the St. Margaret's Bay Road, thirty of whom had left Halifax that morning with their fishing-rods. A considerable number left town, with their rods, in other directions.

6. "Public games are played in many of the streets in fine weather, by crowds of lads and children. Last Sabbath between the hours of 3 and 5 o'clock, p. m , three hundred and forty were so employed,—this is altogether independent

of the hundreds that resort to the Common every Sabbath for a similar purpose.

7. "Last Sabbath, between 3 and 5 o'clock, two hundred and fifty young men were seen standing in groups at the corners of the street and on the Citadel Hill.

8. "Two Public News-rooms were open on Sabbath, and as numerously frequented as on any other day.

9. "Last Sabbath evening, between 8 and 9 o'clock upwards of *eighteen hundred* persons passed Fresh Water Bridge—six hundred and nineteen going down and the rest coming up.

10. "It is computed that not less, on an average, than six hundred cross to Dartmouth every Sabbath, when the weather is fine.

11. "It is computed that not less than five thousand, on an average, are every Sabbath strolling about in the neighborhood of Halifax for pleasure and amusement.

12. "A considerable number of waggons leave Halifax every Sabbath morning on pleasure excursions.

"My Dear Sir, the above I have every reason to believe is correct. There are other forms of Sabbath desecration, but of which I have not yet got any account that can be relied upon.

"I am faithfully yours,
"ALEX. FORRESTER,
"Sec'y H. N. S. S. Alliance.

We shall now leave this branch of our subject, and devote a little special attention to

THE DEVOTEES OF BACCHUS.

In Halifax there abides a brood of Bacchanals, and it is large and pestiferous. It includes individuals of both sexes, who serve their god with constancy and with an idolatrous and brutal delight. The inebriety of this City is woeful; and the misery, wretchedness, degradation, and crime which it breeds baffle the power of language to describe. The temples of Bacchus and of Venus, in Halifax, are neither few nor far between, and these are filled with blind and most degraded worshippers—the extent and enormity of whose wickedness is more than sufficient to call down showers of fire and brimstone, such as once descended upon the Cities of the Plain.

The lukewarm and positively apathetic may smile at these statements, as wild and extravagant, and scoffers may laugh at them outright; nor if so would such be marvellous, seeing many are ignorant of the real moral and spiritual condition of their City, and, worse than this, *love to be so.* But we are not indulging in the hyperbolical, and do not ask credence in mere assertions and unsupported statements. Facts and figures are stubborn things.

Of old this City was noted for its intemperance. When Dr. McGregor came to Halifax, about seventy years ago, he remarked of it that the business of one-half of the people was to sell rum, and of the other half to drink it, and its character for inebriety since that period it has more than sustained. The ratio has been *bad,* worse, *worser,* and what *worst* will be futurity alone will disclose. What *worst* will be, however, if some great reformation does not take place, the *present* does not dimly shadow forth.

According to the Report of the Clerk of License, the number licensed to sell spirituous liquors is two hundred and twenty-seven. The *Provincial Wesleyan Almanack* distributes them thus: 1. Hotels, having bars, 10; 2. Wholesale dealers, not including importers, 12; 3. Retail dealers, with groceries, 119; 4. Confectioneries, 3; 5. Other establishments, 83: Total 227.

Two HUNDRED and TWENTY-SEVEN beings *licensed* to do the work of the Devil! It would be well for the City were there

14

no more employed as caterers for Hell; but some say that the two hundred and twenty-seven may be multiplied by two, to get the sum total of the actual number of those who are professedly and deliberately doing Satan's work. At any rate it is fully fifty per cent more, or THREE HUNDRED AND FOATY.

According to Mr. Morton's Report, in 1859 there were in Albermarle Street forty licensed rum shops, and fully twenty unlicensed; and the proportion of unlicensed to licensed houses is certainly not less than that just stated.

The following, taken from the Police Records, show how the legalized assassins of this City, and their legalizers, work into each others hands: Whole number of arrests by the Police during the last year, 1,630; Drunk, 806; Breaking the Peace, 200; Selling liquor on the Lord's Day, 30; Without license, 19; Drunk, disorderly and fighting, 86; Using obscene and abusive language, 24; Assaulting Police, stabbing, wounding, and breaking windows, 18; Lewd conduct, 30.

When so many were arrested much larger, doubtless, was the number of those who, in numerous instances, eluded the Police, and thus defeated the ends of Justice.

According to the Census of 1861, the number of families in this City is four thousand four hundred and sixty-nine. Admitting that the number of unlicensed Rum Shops is fifty per cent. of the licensed, we have one of them to about every thirteen families; number of Bakeries sixty-nine—one to about sixty-five families. But the most gratifying information of all afforded by the Census returns is, that under the columns for death through "Intemperance," "Poison," and "Murder," there are respectively THREE BLANKS!!

There happened to be only one case of death during the year the Census was taken, and that was only of an old hag, and it was'nt worth while disgracing the Record with it. It was not death either by *intemperance, poison,* or *murder,* but merely *spontaneous combustion!*

"In the early part of the month a woman came to her death by burning, in a house which I visit. The following particulars I received from a man living in the house, and from one of the Coroner's Jury. The woman was an habitual drunkard; she was drunk the night before her death, and the last place she was seen in on the evening she was burned was a *dram shop!* About 10 o'clock the smell of smoke induced a young man passing up stairs to push open the door, when he saw her lying on the floor burning. Help was called, and the fire extinguished; she was quite dead. There was no fire in the fire-place, no fuel, no candle or matches, nor any trace of fire but around the body. The mouth had the appearance as if a flame had issued from it; destroying the lower half of the nose, and burning the upper lip to a cinder. The tongue was also so much burned that the half of it fell out while the body was being washed. The other parts of the face were not disfigured. The young man said the flames had a peculiar appearance, 'sparkling like burning fat.' A bottle was found on the mantle-piece with a little rum in it.

"Her son, a young married man, was sought for, and found so drunk that he could do nothing; and at the funeral next day he was so much intoxicated that he could not walk without being supported by his wife's father."—*Mr. Morton's Report, May,* 1861.

"A woman said to me the other day, with streaming eyes and uplifted hands, Oh! that you could get me to a place where I could not get drink. I have no hope while I am surrounded by it."—*Mr. Morton's Report, Sept.* 2, 1857.

"I would refer to that intolerable nuisance of the City, the handmaid of all wickedness, the *private drinking shop.* To my knowledge, many an inexperienced youth, whom fear, if not shame, deters from the public liquor store, finds in private shops an opportunity to establish a vice which tends to hell. Nor are such places only resorted to by young lads, but young girls, too, may be seen frequenting them.—*Mr. Steele's Report, May* 23, 1856.

" Petty grog sheps are multiplying in many parts of the City; and nearly every brothel keeper is a legalized vender of liquid poison."—*Mr. Morton's Report, Sept.* 2, 1857. '

" On Thursday, 22nd Oct., while pursuing my labors in Barrack Street, I was shown the body of a woman found dead that morning. When discovered she had nothing on her but her under garment and the waist of a dress. The cause of her death was intemperance and debauchery. The licensed houses, where drugged liquors are sold, and which are kept by the worst men in the community, are certainly in the way to hell, going down to the chambers of eternal death. Here the bodies and souls of men are destroyed ; but how few lay it to heart ! "—*Report, Nov.* 4, 1857.

One thing noticeable in the two preceding extracts is this ; —that the furnaces in which men's bodies and souls are destroyed are heated by two fires, viz., by liquid fire and the fire or lust. Victims cast into them have but little chance of escaping alive. Nearly all, sooner or later, are consumed alive. Who care? Not many. The Mayor has publicly declared that *he* cannot even *see* how the progress of destruction and ruin is to be arrested ; and it is a very natural inference that if his vision be not improved he will never *see* that it will be *worth while grappling* with the fell destroyers —inebriety and prostitution. These vices, which walk hand in hand, have now assumed proportions so huge that he can but look on aghast.

The Mayor, in his recent apology for himself and the City Authorities in reference to this point, gave due prominence to the " glorious old principle " that " every man's house is his castle," and, therefore, it cannot be broken in upon by any man, *unless for a commission against* THE LAW ! ! He argued thus :—" We give men a license " to poison men, " but the man who accepts a license has attached to it, as a condition, the right on the part of the Police to enter his premises at any time, and see what is going on,"—a glorious privilege, certainly—"and it is for the sake of having this control that licenses are granted." So, then, a man who has no *permit* to kill other men, may kill and destroy on as large a scale, if he chooses, as the legalized assassin, and yet go scot free? But surely not! Yes; every man's house is his castle. And can it be possible that men without *license* from the City authorities may destroy character, sap the foundations of society, breed poverty, wretchedness, and crime the most appalling, ruin the bodies and souls of men for time and eternity, with impunity? 'Tis even so. On what principle of equity or justice? Just on this principle, that every man's house is his castle; and don't ask any more questions.

Thus, indirectly by connivance and directly by permission, the Civic authorities help on the fiendish work of demoralization and death; and, having done so, as if through some mesmeric influence, they then stand paralized, having only power to exclaim, "Alas! it's horrible! it's heart-rending and fearful beyond description; but, alas! we cannot help it."

"Everybody," says Mr. Sedgewick, in his Lecture on *Amusements for Youth*, "Every body knows the meaning of the phrase, drunk and disorderly; and when this phrase finds its meaning in the opinion of the Watchman, it implies a night's lodging in the Police cell, and a morning's appearance at the Police bar. But these houses bear the stamp of Police authority, and are licensed to sell the very thing that leads to the Police disturbance and the Police punishment. What incongruity in legislation! What a libel on the exercise of authority! What a burlesque on punishment! T license to sell, and then punish the poor wight who bought! To license to sell, and yet lecture the raw, inexperienced, reckless lad, standing with shamed face and dishonored name, in his humiliating plight, against ever being found in such a place again—the place which is kept open and sells its drink

2

by his authority and sanction. Would it not seem that the 'license is granted to minister to the crime lest the magisterial bench should want employment ? "

We think it becomes all who seek the welfare of this community to beseech Almighty God to raise up some—may be poor—" wise man who by his wisdom may deliver the City ; " for here is a " little City, and *few men within it*," and there has come " a great king against it, and besieged it, and built great bulwarks against it," and its chief Magistrate cannot save it, nor see how it is to be saved.

The Rev. Mr. McGregor, in his Lecture, when speaking of the soldiers who arrived from England in the earlier part of the winter, inquired, " How did you feel when you saw them parade your streets? How did you feel again when you saw the same men *drunk*, mad, verging on *delirium tremens?* How would you have felt had you heard the Admiral say, as some of us did, ' It is bad enough that my men on landing should be deluged with rum, but it is *too bad* that they should be *drugged with poison*, and *driven to madness and desertion!*' How would you have felt when a Commanding Officer in one of Her Majesty's Ships inquired, ' Can you direct these men (those who had taken the pledge) to any Sailor's Home or lodging house, where they will not have to contend with the strong-drink temptation ? ' "

Mr. McG. then adds : " By the men themselves some of us have been interrogated; and with mingled feelings of shame and sorrow we were compelled to say ' *We know of none!* ' Shall it continue to be so ? Shall this deep disgrace continue to attach to our city? Our sailors are gone, but the *soldiers* are come; and Oh! what a welcome did they receive in that cold week—our week of Prayer—in January. St. John met them with warm and refreshing beverages. Montreal is now busy preparing a *Temperance*, a *Religious Home* for the brave men who have rushed to the rescue in the hour of peril. Alas! tell it not in Gath, publish it not

in the streets of Ascalen, lest the daughters of the uncircum-
cised should rejoice ; Halifax met them with its usual *fiery
draught*, and DEAD MEN were found on our streets next
morning ! What sad news to go home to mothers and sisters in England ? "

Yes, these caterers for hell, these legalized assassins, who
are doing this work of destruction and death, are the very
beings around whom the civic authorities have thrown the
shield of their protection. So familiar have the citizens generally become with this horrid work, that it is regarded as a
matter of course. Occasionally we meet with a notice in the
papers like this—"That Private John Dodd came to his
death on the night of the 19th inst., by *Alcoholic* poison.
The Jury cannot say from whom he got the rum which caus-
ed his death. The Jury further say that some steps should
be taken by the Civic and Military authorities, to prevent the
sale of such poison, and thus save the lives of many soldiers
in this garrison."

We would suggest the formation of a *Vigilance Committee.* There may be some use in appealing to the Military,
but we see not that anything will be accomplished by apply-
ing to the *Civic* authorities ; for they are evidently in a state
of pitiable decrepitude, with scarcely sufficient ability to keep
Polly Maloney and Billy Bluenose in their places. The following extract, from a *leader* in the *Morning Chronicle*, of
March 13th, shows this pretty clearly :

" Of all the subjects discussed in public, or in private, in
the Legislature or out of it, there is no one, for its importance,
to be compared with that which treats of the management of
the public affairs of this same City of Halifax. The most
sluggish of our citizens—the most apathetic of the dwellers
within the boundaries of the City corporate—will presently
wake up to the discovery of this alarming truth. * * *
That Halifax is rapidly drifting into a state of   embar-
rassment—if not downright bankruptcy—is so plain that only
those who are wilfully blind are insensible to the fact.

Every succeeding year brings with it new and increasing liabilities. Mayor and Aldermen meet day after day, and week after week, and discussion follows discussion, debate, debate, and the end of it all is that Polly Malony is committed for thirty days to Bridewell, or Billy Bluenose is found drunk, reprimanded and recommended to return back to the country; and salaries and taxes continually increase."

* * * * * * * * *

"The public taxes of this City are now about $4.00 for every man, woman and child, within its limits, and are increasing at a rate out of all proportion to its increase in wealth or in population."

So abundant is liquid poison sold in the various forms of *strong drink* in Halifax, that the City is nothing less than a great big Rum shop. Rum on the right hand and rum on the left; rum before you, rum behind you, and rum all round you! Rum *in* the Church and rum *under* the Church! Only think of a Church in this City being literally *founded on a Rum-store!* It is a sight most revolting to any rightly constituted mind.

> "A spirit above and a spirit below,
> A spirit of bliss and a spirit of woe;
> The spirit above is a spirit Divine,
> The spirit below is the spirit of wine."

This verse was found labelled on the Church referred to one morning, having been put on during the night,—the time when ghosts go abroad,—put on no doubt by the patron himself, St. Andrew no less. What think you of that ye uncanonized Churches, destitute of presiding genii, so important as Romish saints? Did a saint of any kind ever give you such a sensible manifestation of his approbation or disapprobation?

When such is the case externally, what will the internal arrangement be? Well, all the Churches in Halifax, we have good reason to believe, are not void of wine-sipping Ministers; and certainly some, if not all of them, have rumtrafficing Elders, members and adherents. The dealers in liquid fire, in some congregations, rank among the quality, and of course the little people would not be so unmannerly as not to doff their hats for the big folk.

In these days of expediency, when peace is at a premium, and purity at a discount, and numbers indispensable, it is at least considered prudent to make a "child's bargain" with those who make merchandise of the bodies and souls of men, women and children. It would be very impolitic to scourge unclean spirits out of the temples. "We know (but this aside and in a whisper), we know that there are men in the Church living upon the moral filth and social degradation of the City, but their money is none the worse for that, and money we must have, no matter how it be raised. We have learned (said boldly) to overcome that squeamishness exhibited under a darker dispensation, which lead those who lived under it to entertain qualms of conscience about putting the ' price of blood ' into the treasury of the Lord."

" Milk for babes, and meat for men." " How do you do, Brother Judas?" " Nicely, thank you kindly, Brother Magus."

" To add to our evils there is *apathy* within the Church at the cry of our perishing Brethren. The cry is still ' Peace! No agitation!' while the world is swimming into perdition, and the Church spotted all over with the contagion. Intemperance has robbed and murdered, ruined families, and destroyed souls, and the Church has been slow to see it, and wash its skirts."—*Rev. P. G. McGregor.*

Murderous poison-vendors in the Church, and sitting at the Lord's table, with their hands full of blood!! " Put them out; put them out; out with them!" cry a hundred individuals; yet, out of that same *hundred* you cannot get *five* willing and ready to lay hands upon them and *put them out.*

But we cannot now pursue further this branch of our subject—though upon its consideration we have but barely entered. We shall need some space for a brief discussion of the third part of the general subject. We would not discharge what we consider a duty—a duty because there are so many "dumb dogs" who will not sound the alarm, and the few who do, do not bark *long* enough nor *loud* enough—in writing this pamphlet, did we shrink from undertaking the very disagreeable work of laying bare, *to some extent,*

"THE SOCIAL EVIL,"

as it is politely termed. We have considered the sin of Sabbath desecration, one woe of the City, and drunkenness, which may be called the second woe-curse, and have come to Prostitution, public and private, which is the most vile and abominable of all, and may be styled the third woe-curse of Halifax.

The libations poured out upon the altar of Bacchus in this City are liquid fires. Vulcan—the brother of this deity—is the god of fire, according to the Greek mythology, and the husband of Venus. Vulcan and Venus (are they not well matched?) are the two great gods which are worshipped in Halifax, and at an enormous expense. But how shall we approach and handle this subject? We must make disclosures fitted to crimson many a cheek,—cheeks of those, we mean, not guilty by actual transgression, for the worshippers of the abominable goddess are as insensible to shame, as they are "dead in trespasses and sin," but we are forced to blush on account of our common humanity. The guilty, we see, have their condemnation branded in their foreheads. Who looks may read. The drunkard, and the prostitute, and the debauchee, have the Cain-mark branded deeply into their brazen brows. Who will arise and, under the Lord, stay the ravages of body an¹ ··¹·destroying evils? Who, with sufficient moral coura. and step in "between the dead and the living?" "Wrath is gone out from the Lord." Who, Phineas like, will arise, take javelins in their hands, pursue the Zimris who go after the Cozbis in this Corinthian City, in the twilight, in the evening, in the black and dark night, "and thrust them through," that "the plague may be stayed?"--Num. xxv. 8. "She hath cast down many wounded; yea, many strong men have been slain by her. Her house is the way to hell going down to the chambers of death."—Prov. vii.

The number of Brothels and of prostitutes, is not known, because of the difficulty of ascertaining it precisely. The number of both, however, is on the increase. Some six or seven years ago the houses of ill-fame were principally confined to the "Hill;" but now they are spread over the City. Old and young, black and white, mothers, sisters, and daughters, are engaged in the horrid commerce. To such an extent is this the case, that parents, in some instances, violate the Divine injunction contained in Leviticus xix. 29.

" The number of prostitutes is increasing in our City, and from the youngest—thirteen or fourteen years—to the eldest, they daily use *strong drink*, to drown alike the voice of conscience and their sorrows."—*Mr. Morton's Report, Feb. 2,* 1859.

Some years ago, one much interested in the fallen women wrote thus : " For several months I have been much grieved and concerned about scores of females who are dying a dreadful death in a part of the city known as " The Hill." I have visited the haunts of vice there, two or three times, and from the mouths of several of them have heard their tales of woe. Several of them had lost their parents when young, and others their characters."

With melancholy sweetness a poor maniac once sang these lines :

> "When lovely woman stoops to folly
> And finds too late that men betray;
> What charm can soothe her melancholy,
> What art can wash her sins away?
>
> "The only art her guilt to cover—
> To hide her shame from every eye:
> To give repentance to her lover,
> And wring his bosom—is to die."

"Some, with tears, could think of nothing but the wrath of God while others were hardened in sin."

According to the Police Returns made some two or three years ago the number of common prostitutes was *five hundred*. According to an estimate made by a Clergyman at a later date there were *six hundred*. Afterwards another Clergyman of the City stated, in a public meeting, that there were as many as five hundred, but many thought the statement extravagant. Subsequently one or two gentlemen of unquestionable authority, who had unusual facilities for ascertaining as nearly as was practicable the actual number, gave, as their opinion, that there were no less than double that number Then we may put the number of the fallen women of this City at ONE THOUSAND.

We have been credibly informed—and we have been very particular as to the source whence we received information—and we mention this circumstance to show that the profligate of the City make no secret of their demoralizing commerce—we were credibly informed that about eighteen months ago a Pimp Establishment removed from the south to another part of the City; and that on their removal the abandoned filled two coaches, which started for the new residence with colors flying!

In addition to the *public*, it is undeniable, though not generally known, that there are many *private* Brothels. Of course the purse-proud and the would-be-thought-to-be-somebody, would not care to meet on common ground Jack Tar and Red Coat.

But we have not the slightest desire to magnify the sins of Halifax ; and notwithstanding all we state we no more than begin to disclose the wickedness and crime, and extent of the social evil of this City. We could scarcly dare to do it, were we able, to its full extent. Yet, how many believe these things are so?

While on this point, we just wish to add—though we are aware that all such disclaimers generally go for very little—that this pamphlet is not written to subserve any selfish end, or gratify any personal feeling, which we think all would feel constrained to acknowledge, if they knew the source whence it has issued. We do not even expect that a sufficient number of copies will sell to pay the expense of publication ; but if the objects for which it has been written, viz: to induce the moral and religion portion of the community to do something more than has been yet attempted to preserve the sanctity of the Lord's day, to suppress public Brothels, to drain off, at least, the floods of Alcoholic poison, and to set in operation benevolent institutions for the redemption of the perishing—if it accomplishes all, or any, of these objects in any degree, we shall never regret having written it, and shall gladly bear the expense of its publication.

As regards the private character of most of the young men of this City, we believe it will not bear a microscopic investigation. The number of unmarried young men between the ages of fifteen and thirteen years—and we may begin with fifteen, because many a boy is a fast young man ere he attains even that age—is two thousand three hundred and seventeen. One half, or at least one thousand, of these we may assume belong to the evangelical denominations of the City ; but how many of these belong to the Young (Old) Men's Christian Association? Said the Rev. Mr. McGregor, in his Lecture, " Excellent laymen connected with this Association assure me that we Ministers *know but little* of the processes of demoralization to which our young men are exposing themselves in large and increasing numbers. Not one hundred, not half that number, resort to your excellent rooms. Not twenty, not ten, will be found at your excellent Prayer Meeting on Saturday night; but the *Restaurants*, if not full, are liberally patronized."

The testimony of those who know best is, that in Halifax vicious young men form the *rule*, the virtuous the *exception*. And we do pity any virtuous young woman who, in double harness, is obliged to trot the journey of life beside a cigar-smoking rake. Rakes! Look out for them. They are numerous, villains at heart, and deceitful as the wind.

"I waive the fact, though I am sorry to do so, that it depraves and brutalizes the ideas and sentiments of young men regarding the place and the functions of woman in society, and unfits and disinclines them for the duties, restraints, obligations and holy delights of the married state. Oh! lust is not love, as your vile sensualist would teach us, and it would be a moral miracle indeed to find your systematic seducer, or your weekly frequenter of the brothel and the stew, the companion of the bawd and the slave of the whore, a devoted husband, a wise and kind father, content and satisfied with the pleasures of home."—*Rev. R. Sedgewick.*

"That drunkeness and prostitution are on the increase is undeniable; and I fear there are few who sigh and cry before God, on account of the abominations done in our midst."— *Mr. Morton's Report, Oct. 2, 1861.*

They are on the increase because money-making.

"Many of these depraved haunts are kept by white married people as their source of livlihood, and from which source some of them have saved considerable sums of money."— *Mr. Steele's Report, Dec. 31, '55.*

The more deeply the matter is probed the blacker it becomes. Mark the following:—"These poor immortal souls are daily becoming more reckless of the past and careless of the future. * * And how can this but be when men, calling

themselves Christians—to impeach which cognomen would be
a grave offence—when men, professing Christiany * * *
are on the one hand spending their money to sustain and en-
courag. .. miserable outcasts; and on the other hand receiving the rents of their houses out of the wages of iniquity."—*Mr. Steele's Report, July 2, '56·*

There it is. Just take a good look at it. Men occupy-
ing *respectable (?)* positions receiving rent out of the wages
of iniquity! To what will men not stoop for filthy lucre?
Only think of an Alderman, and an *Elder* having a house
rented as a *Brothel!* What are we coming to? Only think
of a moral scavenger of that kind handing round at the
Lord's table, the symbols of the broken body and shed blood
of Jesus Christ!

We do not wish to be invidious, but we take Presbyterians
as examples, because they pique themselves upon the effici-
ency of their Church Government and Discipline. Let us,
then, take another *Elder* as a specimen. An Elder, then,
will go to the Union Prayer-Meeting, preside or offer a
prayer in common with others, proceed from the meeting to a
wharf where he finds some casks of what has been aptly
called "distilled damnation," inserts his spirit-detector into
them, takes it out, tastes, and addressing the by-standers,
says, "Just taste this, gentlemen, and see how good it is;
just take a little and you will bid all the better." And let
it be borne in mind that these are not poetic descriptions, or
creations of the imagination, but representations of living
verities. So now with David we can only say—"It is time
for thee to work, Lord, for they have made void thy law."
But Matthew Henry informs us that the passage, without
doing violence to the original, may be read thus,—"It is
time to work for thee, Lord, for they have made void thy
law." God will work, just as he is now working in the neigh-
bouring Republic, when this City's cup of iniquity is full.
Even the *form* of godliness—not to make any mention of

decency—is beginning to depart from our midst. Oh, who would stand in these men's shoes when the Lord shall be revealed from heaven in flaming fire?

Save the fallen, do we pray? "Speak unto the people that they go forward." Imagine such a prayer as this being offered to God:—

"Lord, raise the fallen, and save the degraded. Do so, we beseech thee, only relieve us from the unpleasantness of soiling our fingers in lifting them up out of the deep, deep ditch into which they are fallen.

"As for us, thy ministers, we preach two sermons a week to our flocks. That we may do our work more effectually we exercise much caution. We don't make rude assaults upon men's consciences. We begin our discourses some distance off, and then by a circular movement preach ourselves near them. Thus by working all round them, when we don't begin at too great a distance, we succeed in touching those parts which jut out more prominently. It would never do to go right at them, cutting right and left with the sword of the spirit, for many of thy professed people have become very crotchety in these latter days, and this being the case we find it *expedient* to curry them down. If we did not do so they would stop our pay, and then church affairs would soon come to a dead lock.

"We visit the families of our flocks. But we have to confess that when we get comfortably seated down in their drawing-rooms we too often forget those who live in cells, prisons, cellars and garrets, in the high-ways, by-ways and hedges. But we don't altogether forget these for we employ a servant of thine to carry the Gospel to the poor, the halt, the maimed and the blind. Times have greatly changed since the Master was on earth. We have fallen upon fashionable, tho' fastidious days, and know not how else we could save ourselves and thy cause from reproach, and at the same time preserve our own dignity.

"And as 'the laborer is worthy of his hire,' we pay thy servant £100 annually for his valuable services. For this sum we are indebted to the generosity of the people. Their liberality, too, is considerable; inasmuch as about £90 of the amount is given by some 120 or 130 donors, and the balance raised by collections taken in various churches. Sometimes the sum total amounts to £123 or more.

" A few years ago our sympathies were much drawn out towards the fallen women of our city. The result was that we prepared for them an asylum, by which, under thy blessing, several were benefitted, some reclaimed, and restored to their husbands and society, and, best of all, some were led to the Saviour,—and all within three years. After this, and with shame and confusion of face we confess it, our love for the perishing declined apace, and the Refuge failed and became *non est* the third or fourth year after it had been established.

" But the multitude of the perishing around remind us that we are required to be abundant in works of faith and labors of love, so having recruited, after a rest of four or five years, we are now thinking of erecting a 'Sailor's Home.' We fear, however, if we do establish an institution of this kind that we shall but amuse ourselves with it for two or three years, and then drop it, like the House of Refuge, for something more novel."

We sometimes fear we may unadvisedly offend some of the children of God by our remarks. Believe us, it would be a strong inducement that would lead us to say one disrespectful word against the servants of the Most High. It is not because we love you the less we thus speak, but because we commiserate the perishing the more. We shall now take the liberty of asking you one or two questions, and then leave you to your own reflections :—Have you done all you ought, all you can, and all you intend to do for the amelioration of the moral condition of the thousands who are miserably perishing around you?

How great is the drowsiness and spiritual deadness of the professing people of God in this city! Is it obvious and palpable? Let Prayer Meetings—the denominational and the Union—answer.

But Oh, would it not move a heart of adamant to hear wretched captives, slaves in bondage, delivered over to the brutal passions of brutal, inhuman monsters, in the form of men—to hear down-trodden women, degraded as women never were in heathen lands, to hear them sighing for deliverance—for a deliverance withheld by the christian philanthropists of Halifax?

Under date Nov. 3, 1858, Mr. Morton writes: "A few appear thankful for the attention paid them, and confess that they sometimes feel bitterly their sad degradation, and have a desire to reform. But when they enquire, 'What shall we do? We cannot reform here, and nobody will take us in.' I confess I hardly know what to say." No wonder, Mr. Morton; a few sympathize with you. The women reason well. There is no earthly chance for them so long as they remain where they are; and where they are they must remain until an asylum be provided for them.

It is indeed trying to be non-plussed in that way; but though the City Missionary may not know how to answer such interrogatories, rest assured God knows how to dispose of those who see others "drawn unto death and forbear to deliver them." Only think of the Institution for fallen women which was in operation in this City for some years, and which accomplished much good, languishing and dying—not for want of inmates, but lacking *a few pounds* to keep it up! What a reproach! "Let the sighing of the prisoner come before thee; according to the greatness of thy power preserve thou those that are appointed to die; and render unto our neighbours sevenfold into their bosom their reproach wherewith they have reproached thee, O Lord."—Psalm lxxix. 11, 12.

"A few days ago," writes Mr. M., Feb. 2, '59, "I met a poor creature in the street, with a shawl over her head. She stopped me and said—'Mr. M. I suppose you don't know me.' I answered, 'No.' 'I am Harriet ———, that you so often talked to in the House of Refuge,' &c." Mr. Morton adds, "She was very much altered, and complained bitterly of having been turned abroad when the House of Refuge was closed."

How trying to the faith and generous feelings of the Missionary! What could he say, but, "May God assist you, poor hapless girl. With sighs and tears I bewail your parental and moral orphanage. I have been striving to enlist the sympathies of the Lord's professed people in this City on your behalf, but alas! in vain: God alone can move their sluggish souls."

"In conversing with the inmates of these houses some express themselves as being unhappy and desirous of reformation."—*Report, Feb.* 4, 1857.

"The reformation of a young woman gives me much pleasure. She is about nineteen, good looking and intelligent. About a year ago she was drawn aside from the paths of virtue by bad company. By frequenting places of ill repute she was likely to be ruined. She is an orphan, and has no friends here but the woman with whom she lived. I endeavored to save her by advice, and by calling at the houses she frequente and warning them against harboring her. All my efforts appeared to be in vain, till last autumn, when she awoke to a sense of her awful situation. She at once gave up her habit and companions, and removed to Boston, to avoid temptation, and has ever since done well. She lives with a pious family, earns her livelihood by her needle, and manifests seriousness of mind."—*Report, June* 1, 1859.

"In one of my visits to a house in Barrack Street, a young woman expressed herself as heartily weary of her present life, and desirous of returning to the paths of virtue; from her appearance she had not been long in her present course. She is a native of the eastern part of the Province, and named persons as relatives whom I know to be respectable characters. I was sorry I could do nothing for her but counsel her."—*Report, April* 3, 1861.

Now, if the men of the City cannot be moved to noble deeds, in Heaven's name let us appeal to the women. Woman!—Have "you shut up your bowels of compassion" against the down-trodden of your sex? It cannot be so. It is not so. But you have not set about realizing the extent of the misery and degradation of the fallen. Were a tithe of the scenes of sin, suffering, and sorrow daily occurring in this City to pass before you in panoramic vision, your bosoms would heave with sighs, your souls swell with sadness, and the scenes sour your sweetest cups.

Much is to be done : who are to do it? and when is it to be done? The wicked are strengthening each other's hands, while in some things the righteous do not co-operate among themselves. Sometimes they are found working against each other, as was the case on the evening Rev. Mr. McGregor lectured on the " Moral wastes of the City," &c. It is our impression that while vice is daily gaining ground in Halifax, the actual moral force of the city is becoming less and weaker. If so, let this state of matters run on without interruption as has been the case for the last few years, and in a short time the moral and God-fearing will be utterly unable to cope with abounding and multiplying iniquity. We wonder what would be effectual in leading the well-disposed of this city to see their danger, and promptly respond to the alarm—To arms ! To arms !

The indifference manifested is alarming. Many circumstances concur to show this. For one example take Mr. McGregor's lecture, from which we have already given extracts (and here we would thankfully acknowledge our obligation to gentlemen who allowed us the use of papers from which important information has been derived). That lecture was fitted to awaken to a feeling of danger, and arouse to a sense of duty. The occasion on which it was delivered was not very favorable, we admit, but it turned out a star-light night, and the streets were quite passable. When the hour for opening the meeting arrived there were only about fifty persons present; but ere the Lecturer closed, the spacious Hall was comfortably filled with about two hundred individuals. The platform was adorned by *one* Pastor of a congregation and his Assistant, and *two* Preachers. And what did all that mean? Was the Lecturer unpopular? Not by any means; but unfortunately HIS SUBJECT WAS.

The next Lecture—a good one—was on the *mysterious*, and drew more than double the audience, who found their way to the Hall in a starless night and through miry streets, guided thither no doubt by curiosity, and the friendly assistance of lamp-posts—which, by the way, in Halifax, are not unlike "angels' visits."

"Three points," says the City Missionary, in his report, for 1855, "I may allude to, of which I have had such proofs as to amount in my case to a solemn conviction: First, The spiritual drowsiness and ignorance of Scripture that pervade the Protestant Episcopal Church of England people. Secondly, The immense amount of stupid idolatry, superstition and sin, in which the Catholic is steeped. Thirdly, The extension of Universalism and Mormonism, which, with practical Atheism, seem to characterize the great body of the community."

The Missionary's first point is probably impartial, for Mr. Steele received Episcopal ordination previou his leaving Halifax But if the Episcopalians were drowsy in 1855, they, we fear, together with numbers in all the other evangelical denominations of this City, have since fallen asleep, and now are all napping it out quite comfortably.

As to his second point, it is certainly true and well expressed; for in this year of our Lord 1862, persons in this City, and these not the least intelligent, will tell you, with all the seriousness and credulity imaginable, of a lady, who, having put a consecrated wafer in her mouth, and then apply-

3

ing a handkerchief to her lips took it away covered with gore. Pretty strong stomach for a lady!

Witness, too, St. Patrick's night processions of from 500 to 1000 individuals—many of these having their faces blackened, and otherwise disguised—patrolling the streets at midnight, carrying torches, and hobbling along to the sound of old screeching fifes, drums, or old tin pans. To corroborate this notice let us summon their spokesman. The following is from the *Evening Express*, of March 17th—Pat's own day —and written under this caption, "The Festival of St. Patrick."

"The anniversary of the patron saint of Ireland (this day) was ushered in by one of the most fearful storms of the season. * * * * Notwithstanding all these drawbacks on the outward hilarity incidental to the festival of St. Patrick, not a few of the votaries of his saintship were 'out' at the midnight, certainly not the witching, hour, and with the aid of music ushered in the returning anniversary. Even these strong-limbed enthusiastic fellows must have found Jordon a hard road to travel on indeed."

What a ludicrous notice of a barbarous festival! There is just as must need to send the Gospel to these poor blind people as to painted savages in the South Sea Islands.

"Heathens abroad, and heathens at home;
Not far is the need for your mission to roam;
Our highways and by-ways, the streets and the lanes,
Claim the first care, and will yield the first gains."

We shall now enquire—What is the state of Halifax in an educational point of view? and what is being done towards instructing the ignorant and elevating the degraded? In this City there are 4,836 persons over five years of age who cannot read; and 5,864 who cannot write. *Twenty-four per cent.* of the entire population are illiterate! "*One fourth* of the families are *crammed* into cellars and garrets, and single rooms, where industry and morality are all but impossible. We have become accustomed to regard this PERISHING CLASS as the natural and inevitable residium of society. A large part of our population is *sinking* instead of rising, and *will sink lower still*, unless Christian people of the City are awakened and induced to work in another manner and with greater zeal, unanimity and diligence than we have hitherto displayed."

How many Ragged Schools are there in Halifax? One, and its history has been eventful. This benevolent Institution was established in 1852, and has been in operation ever since, excepting on those occasions when unavoidable interruptions occurred, such as when the stove-pipe needed repairs, or a freshet arose, &c.

" The Ragged School has been closed for a short time owing to the overflowing of the water on the premises." *Mr. Morton's Report*, March 2, 1859. Subsequently, as this was a periodical inundation, the School embarked and set sail for Africa. " The Ragged School has been removed to the African School-room." *Report* Feb. 5, 1862.

So much for the philanthropy c. the wealthiest city in the Lower Provinces of B. N. America.

Any Reformatories for Inebriates? None. Any Soldier's Home? None. Any Sailor's Homes? None; but there is one Old Woman's Home. Any Houses of Refuge? None. Well, what is there in Halifax? The City Father's Rum-poison sheps—two or three of them—under the Market House.

The following shows how these functionaries subserve each others' interests :—An Alderman keeps a rum-shop. A man goes in, becomes fuddled, is turned out on the street, a Policeman picks him up and lugs him off to the Police Court. The Mayor sends him to jail with to the work-house where he remains a few days, gets out, returns to the Alderman's, gets drunk again, is again turned out, taken to the Mayor, sent to Bridewell, etc.

Boston has 180,000 inhabitants, and 1904 Rum shops, that is one shop for about every 94 persons. Halifax 25,000 inhabitants, and 340 Rum-poison shops; that is one shop for every 73 individuals. But if the Civic authorities think the Rum-poison is a good thing, why not provide an abundant supply ?

In 1854 a House of Refuge for fallen females was opened. During the first year it had 11 inmates, and the Committee of that year reported that they believed "only one returned to a life of shame." On the 1st January, 1855, the House contained five who professed a desire to reform. During the year ten more were received. Of these

"Two were sent to the Poor's Asylum, being deficient in intellect; one sent at her own request to friends in Scotland; two went to service, and did well—one was led astray by intemperance; one never left the house, was obedient, industrious, and attentive to religious instruction; four in the house, obedient and industrious; three left without the Committee's approval, of whom two left Halifax and got situations as servants; one, being a married woman, returned to her husband; one was married in the house; one may be found in the workhouse, having fallen through the love of strong drink."

The House, No. 20 Lockman Street was not a suitable one, because it was in an exposed position, and farther, because two or more of the inmates were obliged to occupy a single room, and for other reasons. Such at least was the opinion of the matron. The premises were rented or £40 per annum. Notwithstanding all these drawbacks, the Institution proved a blessing to several.

"The whole expenditure for the year (1855)
          amounts to.......................£280 1 7.
Receipts including Legislative grant,.......161 9 11."

The following was published two and a half years after the House was opened :—

"The Institution has now been over two and a-half years in operation, during which time it has afforded protection, relief and instruction—useful and spiritual—to twenty-nine persons. Of that number, eleven afford strong ground of encouragement to the Committee; several having gone to service in families of respectability, where they receive Christian care;

three to the houses of Clergymen, others to distant parts of the country to their own relatives; leaving only two of this class in the House, who, though not many months inmates, give good promise of the future. Many of these, too, have from time to time written to the Superintendent, expressing gratitude to Almighty God and the Committee for the benefit which they derived during their abode at the House. And of this division, too, it is worthy of remark that nearly all, often expressed the hope ' that they would not be removed from the House of Refuge, unless to places where they would be under proper restraint and religious instruction ;' and two of their number proved the sincerity of this their hope and purpose of amendment, by leaving places where *Drink* and *Irreligion* placed them in temptation,—and returned again with thankfulness to the Asylum. Of the remaining eighteen, the Superintendent speaks in hopeful terms of SIX, one of whom is still an inmate, and, although their advancement is not so satisfactory as might be wished, still there is amendment ; and the Committee in dependance upon the Divine blessing humbly desiring to do good to all, and beside all waters to scatter the life-giving Word of Christ, cast this burden upon the merciful Saviour, and prayerfully look for and await his blessing. The remaining twelve have been removed from the House under unfavorable circumstances — it being one of the Rules of the Establishment that the incorrigible, who set a bad example to others, cannot be retained. * * *

" The present appeal becomes necessary to the existence of the Institution, as will appear by the abstract of its pecuniary affairs, as follows:—January, 1854, to July, 1856, total amount received on behalf of the House of Refuge, including the Provincial grant, £50, two last years. as also the sum of £22 10s., earned by the inmates as work offered, £727 19s. 5d. Same time, paid: Furniture £31 10s., Salary Superintendent, £105, Rent £100, Clothing £40, Printing and Sundries £25, Fuel £35—£336 10s. Balance—for provisions of inmates and Superintendent's family, being £156 11s. 8d. per annnum—£391 9s. 5d.

"And when it is borne in mind that the subscription raised in 1855 amounted to only £111 9s. 10d., it cannot be matter of surprise that a debt of £118 11s. 8d. should appear against the subscription of the present year, and that consequently the Treasurer's account balanced on the 1st July.

From this simple state of facts, the Committee confidently appeal to the Christian public to come forward and sustain an Institution of whose usefulness, both to Society at large and personally to the poor objects of its fostering care, eternity alone will reveal the extent. The Directors feel, too, that the public should be put in possession of the awful fact, that a number of persons in this City make their living by inveigling from their homes *young, inexperienced girls;* and when it is added that since its commencement the Refuge has been the blessed instrument, in the hands of God, of rescuing *two,* both under fifteen years of age, from the destroyer, and placing them at service in Christian families, before guilt had debased the mind and seared the conscience, they feel confident that such a claim has been established as entitles them to public support in their effort, and so by placing their Treasurer in a position to call in the subscriptions falling due in January, 1857, *free of debt,* at once invest their undertaking with the character of permanency—a blessing to the City for future years. P. G. McGregor, *Secretary.*

JOHN STEELE, *Chaplain.*"

After all the good accomplished by that excellent Institution in so short a time and under many disadvantages, the spirited, magnanimous, noble, philanthropic Christians of Halifax allowed it to languish and die *three* years after it was founded. Hear its death-knell tolled in January, 1857.

"*Extract of Minutes of Committee held at Mr. Ritchie's Office, Jan. 27th* 1857 :—The Directors spent some time in considering the state of their finances, prospects for 1857, the results of the experiment so far, and particularly whether the good flowing from the Refuge was such as to warrant the Directors in calling upon the public for the funds necessary for its support. P. G. McGregor, *Sec'ty.*"

How strongly that savors of avarice, not to say anything about the smack of infidelity! Ah! if they had only been as good at making calculations about the value of A SOUL as they were at those of pounds, shillings, and pence, how different would have been the result!

Compare the success of the Halifax Refuge with that of Boston :

" During the last year (1853) the Magdalenes in the Boston Asylum numbered twelve ; the average for several years being fifteen ; although it has been in operation since 1823 ; possesses ample accommodations and appliances for benefitting such as may flee to it for refuge ; and is surrounded by a population many times greater than that of Halifax.—*Report of Com. H. of R.*, 1854.

We shall close our remarks en'this topic by giving a c⁰py of a letter, which was addressed to the Matron of the Institution by one of the reclaimed. In our opinion the letter, as to the conception of its sentiments, would do honor to one of much higher pretensions.

" HALIFAX, March 31, 1856.

" *Dear Mrs. W*——,—As I am to leave the City shortly, I consider it a privilege to address a few lines to you, expressive of my gratitude to you for all your kindness and sympathy towards me. They only who have suffered as I have can tell how much good a kind word can do those who are burdened with sorrow. I thank you for your maternal counsels, your religious instructions, and attention to my bodily wants. These have contributed to *lighten* my sorrows, to *re-kindle* my hopes, and *point* to that Friend who sticketh closer than a brother ; who receiveth sinners when all others forsake them, who has taught me to see the error of my ways, and I trust who will lead me in the paths of righteousness for His name's sake.

" I thank the ladies and gentlemen of the Committee for the interest they have manifested in my welfare. I thank the City Missionaries for their watchful care over me, and earnestly do hope that their prayers in my behalf may be attended with blessings to their souls and my own ; for ' he that watereth shall himself be watered.' I hepe that many others will avail themselves of the benefit of the Institution, and you will not have to complain that you have spent your strength for *nought*. And I assure you, with much esteem, I remain, dear Mrs. W——, your obedient and humble servant, MARY A. C——."

Ladies of Halifax, will you not re-establish the House of Refuge, that noble Institution, and thus roll away the reproach

brought upon the Christian portion of the community by those
who allowed it to die? Do, and God will bless you; and
posterity will arise and call you blessed. Do not forget either
that there are many around you — not altogether outcasts—
but those who have been thrown upon the cold charities of a
heartless world, with none to care either for their bodies or
their souls. Take the following as an example :—

One day a gentleman entered a poor cabin in this city. It
was a wintry day, but there was not a spark of fire on the
cold hearth stone, nor fuel enough to make one. The mother
of a little family was under the influence of strong drink.
Though wretched-looking, there was a something in her coun-
tenance which evoked his sympathies and enlisted his prepo-
sessions Her tale of woe was a moving one. Two or three
months previous she had given birth to two children, and both
were dead. What a world, he thought, upon which those
infants opened their eyes. What a reception I Not one com-
fort of life was there in that miserable abode. Freely the
tears poured forth with which her face was soon suffused.
Woman's tears! If weeping women's tears shed over blight-
ed hopes, broken vows, and desolated homes were all congealed
they would form a mountain high upon which angels might
descend and also weep.

Poor body! she had been obliged to earn her daily bread,
when, in the natural course of events, she should have been
enjoying ease, a circumstance which did not diminish her sorrows in her hour. As she used to lay upon her uncomfortable
bed, after the burial of her infants, a little boy would come
near and say, " Mother, why do you cry ?' but the artless
question would not seal the fountain of her tears. Thereupon
that little fellow would be sent for some *strong drink*, of
which a draught would be taken to hush over-wrought feelings,
and drown accumulating sorrows.

Now, will not tales such as these, which are but specimens
of many untold, evoke a sympathetic response from woman's

tender heart? We hope so, at least. No case need be despaired of. Strong drink had beggared that family, but one of its heads, after a few unsuccessful attempts, overcome the habit of taking its destroying draughts. Great was the change produced in her domestic arrangements by that victory. Her cabin from being a drunken abode was transformed into a tidy home. Helped and encouraged by a little friendly assistance, so much has been accomplished, under the blessing of God, and by his grace she bids fair to overcome the world, the flesh and the devil. Then despise not the fallen. By the unmeritted favor of God ye are what ye are.

Christian ladies of Halifax, will you arise and in the majesty of your might save the " Black Town." * Will you enter upon the noblest of enterprises, that of being co-workers with God, in checking rolling tears as they chase each other down woman's wan cheek, in filling up channels ploughed long and deep, in cheering desponding hearts, and turning wretched into peaceful happy homes? Home is not in the vocabulary of the drunkard. Home! the fallen of your sex have none. Shall it always be so in Halifax? Your presence in many a cell, cellar and garret would be like the breaking in of light into a dark place. Will you, then, enter upon the noblest of enterprises, seeking and saving the lost? The field is large and inviting The life most pleasing to God is that which is the most beneficial to mankind. Will you begin anew, and with a right good will, work for God? Every Christian woman's heart in unison responds—"We will. We will, and at once, for woman's sake, for the city's sake, and above and beyond all, for JESUS' sake." Amen.

* A name given to Halifax by foreigners.